Seed Surprise

Story by Regine Fanning, R.S.M.
Illustrations by Tianna Pagels

I have a seed.
It is little.

It is black and hard.
Something is in it.

**Is it something big?
Maybe a pumpkin.
I could make a jack-o-lantern.**

Mom could bake a pie.
Is it something little?
What is in my seed?

Is it something tall?
Maybe an apple tree.

**Is it something small?
Maybe a pink flower.**

What is in my seed?
A surprise for me!